Suffering is not generic. It is partic
and to their personal stories. Esthe
ful devotional about the trial of chrc
by her story but also resonates beyc   ...p.......... because it
winsomely draws from the fathomless fountain of biblical truth
and gospel celebration. The best thing I can say about this book
is that is speaks eloquently to chronic illness but also gives hope
and wisdom for all sufferers and for those who seek to care for
them as well.

    —**Andy Farmer**, Pastor of Counseling and Care, Covenant
        Fellowship Church, Glen Mills, Pennsylvania; Author, *Real*
        Peace: What We Long For and Where to Find It

Esther Smith's devotional on chronic illness is simply outstand-
ing. As one who struggles with pain every minute of every day, I
need to be reminded of the hope I have in Jesus. This devotional
delivers an avalanche of hope as well as practical help about how
to care for our bodies. Read this devotional, and then reread it
again and again. It will bless your body and soul.

    —**Dave Furman**, Senior Pastor, Redeemer Church of Dubai;
        Author, *Being There: How to Love Those Who Are Hurting*
        and *Kiss the Wave: Embracing God in Your Trials*

Finally, a devotional that gives a validating voice to the suffering
of chronic illness while also bringing essential hope and purpose
through the life-giving promises of Scripture. Esther's empathetic
words capture the pains, sorrows, joys, and victories that come
when we understand that God uses illness for his glory. You will
no longer suffer alone as you take up the journey of walking with
God in the pages of this book.

    —**Eliza Huie**, Director of Counseling, McLean Bible Church,
        DC Metropolitan Area; Dean of Biblical Counseling, Metro
        Baltimore Seminary

Chronic Illness: Walking by Faith is an exceptional devotional written by one who understands chronic illness, who has experienced its life-changing impact, and who leans deeply into Jesus. Esther offers no quick answers; instead, she invites us to engage with Scripture, to read her honest thoughts about a life that she didn't expect but longs to steward well, and to consider thoughtful reflection questions and action steps. A feast to savor and treasure!

—**Cindee Snider Re**, Cofounder, Chronic Joy (chronic illness ministry); Author, Chronic Joy Thrive Series and Abide Series

Esther Smith is a caring and compassionate friend who understands the tiresome challenges of living with chronic illness. Reading this devotional, and following its wise and gracious counsel, will clear your mind, strengthen your heart, and grow your faith.

—**Paul Tautges**, Senior Pastor, Cornerstone Community Church, Mayfield Heights, Ohio; Founder, *Counseling One Another* (blog)

CHRONIC ILLNESS

31-Day Devotionals for Life

A Series

Deepak Reju
Series Editor

CHRONIC ILLNESS

WALKING BY FAITH

ESTHER SMITH

P U B L I S H I N G
P.O. BOX 817 • PHILLIPSBURG • NEW JERSEY 08865-0817

Library of Congress Cataloging-in-Publication Data

Names: Smith, Esther (Biblical Counselor), author.
Title: Chronic illness : walking by faith / Esther Smith.
Description: Phillipsburg, New Jersey : P&R Publishing, 2020. | Series: 31-day devotionals for life | Includes bibliographical references. | Summary: "Biblical counselor Esther Smith shows how the gospel enables people with illness to release   guilt and shame, balance work and rest, and get through difficult days."-- Provided   by publisher.
Identifiers: LCCN 2019048200 | ISBN 9781629956886 (paperback) | ISBN 9781629956893 (epub) | ISBN 9781629956909 (mobi)
Subjects: LCSH: Suffering--Religious aspects--Christianity. | Suffering--Prayers and devotions. | Chronic pain--Religious aspects--Christianity.
Classification: LCC BV4910 .S65 2020 | DDC 248.8/6--dc23
LC record available at https://lccn.loc.gov/2019048200

Contents

Tips for Reading This Devotional

EARLY IN OUR MARRIAGE, my wife and I lived on the top floor of a town house, in a small one-bedroom apartment. Whenever it rained, leaks in the roof would drip through the ceiling and onto our floors. I remember placing buckets in different parts of the apartment and watching the water slowly drip, one drop at a time. I put large buckets out and thought, *It'll take a while to fill them.* The water built up over time, and often I was surprised at how quickly those buckets filled up, overflowing if I didn't pay close enough attention.

Like rain filling up a bucket, this devotional will surprise you. It may not seem like much; just a few verses every day. Drip. Drip. Drip. Yet a few drops of Scripture daily can satiate your parched soul. The transformative power of these readings will build over time and overflow into your life.

Why does a book like this make such a difference?

We start with Scripture. God's Word is powerful. Used by the Holy Spirit, it turns the hearts of kings, brings comfort to the lowly, and gives spiritual sight to the blind. It transforms lives and turns them upside down. We know that the Bible is God's very own words, so we read and study it to know God himself.

Our study of Scripture is practical. Theology should change how we live. It's crucial to connect the Word with your struggles. Often, as you read this devotional, you'll see the word *you* because Esther speaks directly to you, the reader. The readings contain a mixture of reflection questions and practical suggestions. You'll get much more from this experience if you answer the questions and do the practical exercises. Don't skip them. Do them for the sake of your own soul.

Our study of Scripture is worshipful. When you are experiencing a chronic illness, many days are hard. The pain, fatigue, lack of energy, guilt and shame, reduced engagement with your friends or church—all of it can overrun your life. Yet it doesn't have to. In the middle of your pain, where do you turn? Away from God or to him? Is it easy for us to turn to God when we're overrun by pain and heartache? No—it's incredibly hard. Some days, it feels impossible. But this is our goal—to run to Christ and to live by faith through our suffering. So we spend our time in God's Word to help ourselves to worship the King of our hearts—Christ. Our bodies may waste away, our minds may struggle to concentrate, our lack of energy may leave us stuck at home or missing yet another church service, but we cling to the refuge of our souls— our Savior, Jesus.

If you find this devotional helpful (and I trust that you will!), reread it in different seasons of your life. Work through it this coming month, and then come back to it a year from now, to remind yourself how to persevere through chronic illness. You'll also find additional resources at the end of the book to help you as you continue your journey.

That's enough for now. Let's begin.

Deepak Reju

Introduction

I WALKED INTO the Johns Hopkins rheumatology department feeling defensive. Over the past ten years, I had seen a string of rheumatologists, and every single time, the appointment had ended in discouragement. This time, my shields were up. I was not letting another indifferent doctor hurt me again.

Things did not go as I anticipated. From the beginning, this appointment was different. The doctor took great care as he reviewed my history. He asked about my current symptoms and completed an extensive physical exam. Then he sat down on his stool, looked at me, and said, "So, tell me what brings you here today. What are you concerned about?"

My mind raced. I was concerned about a lot of things that were happening to my body; but in that moment, I was most concerned about what he was going to say. If I heard one more doctor tell me I was fine, I might scream. My answer was curt—fueled by years of dismissal and unexplained symptoms. "I didn't even want to come today! I'm sure I'm fine. I'm only here because my other doctor told me to come."

I looked down at my lap, waiting for him to say there was nothing he could do for me. Instead, he got straight to the point. "You have lupus. Your physical exam also indicates that you have hypermobility syndrome."

"What? No . . . seriously?"

This was unexpected. I had known that lupus was a possibility for some time but had never thought I would be diagnosed. After over a decade of searching for answers, I finally knew the cause of all my symptoms.

In the weeks following that pivotal doctor's appointment, so much of my life began to make more sense. Since childhood, I had experienced flare-ups of symptoms that would come and go and then come back again months or years later. I had suffered through unexplained fatigue, and although it was hard to put into words, my body never felt quite right. My most challenging symptom was chronic pain that was related to a chiropractic injury six years earlier. The hypermobility syndrome provided a partial explanation for why this injury had happened in the first place and why I struggled to recover.

These physical symptoms had been just the tip of the iceberg for me. Following my chiropractic injury, my physical abilities had deteriorated until I was forced to spend most of each day lying down. My life became very small, which took a heavy toll on my emotions and sense of self. I struggled to go to work and keep up with daily tasks of living. I struggled to make and keep friends and to be in community. I felt anxious and sad, angry and defeated. I cried a lot. Life felt meaningless, and I didn't think things would ever get better.

For a long time, I felt alone in this experience. Now I know that there are millions of other people with chronic illness. Over the years, I have met many of them. Although we all struggle in different ways, our experiences share one similar quality: Our illnesses are persistent. They last months into years into lifetimes. More than anything else, this is what makes chronic illness hard. From arthritis to chronic migraines, from diabetes to Crohn's disease, chronic illness comes and it doesn't go away.

Maybe chronic illness has been part of your story since birth. Or perhaps it interrupted your life at what seemed like the worst possible time. Your symptoms could be a minor inconvenience, or they may have devastated all your dreams and plans. No matter your particular circumstances, you have likely grieved and doubted, wondered and questioned. Emotions have overwhelmed you. Fears have enveloped you. The future looms as a frightening unknown. Will you ever get better? What good could possibly come from your pain?

I know you may have struggled to get out of bed this morning. Or maybe you long for just one meal that won't make your body revolt. You might be exhausted beyond words—weary and ready for bed by midafternoon. But after years or decades, just when it seems things will never change, many people find that they do. Sometimes we find solutions that take our symptoms away. Other times, change happens inside us. *We* change. We grow. We learn better ways to approach being sick.

Learning to live with chronic illness happens through trial and error. We learn as we talk to people who have more years of illness behind them than we do. Most importantly, we learn as we read Scripture and consider what God has to say about physical suffering. And that is what this book is about.

This devotional is divided into four sections that highlight four lessons Scripture has taught me about how to faithfully live with chronic illness. As you continue to read, I hope you are surprised by how much Scripture has to say about chronic illness. I hope you see that Scripture can change what you believe about chronic illness and that this can truly make a difference.

Perhaps the most important lesson I have learned is that chronic illness can take away many things, but it can never take away God's presence. This doesn't mean we will always *feel* God's presence. It does mean that even when you feel forgotten and alone, God is with you. When you are overwhelmed with sorrow, God invites you to tell him how much it hurts. When life doesn't offer any answers, God offers you himself. The first lesson is this: *Draw near to God, because he is your only certainty.*

I have also learned that God invites people who live with chronic illness to make self-care a priority. When you have a chronic illness, taking care of yourself can become all-consuming. You may spend most of each day taking care of your body, managing the emotional and mental toll of your illness, navigating relationships, and maintaining faith during hard times. Spending so much time on self-care can feel selfish or meaningless to some people, but this work is well worth your time. *Take care of yourself, because God is glorified when you faithfully care for the body and soul he has given you.*

Another lesson I have learned is that God often uses the unique circumstances of people who have chronic illness to further his kingdom. I used to think that my illness was a spiritual liability because it kept me from doing so many things. I now know that physical limitation can become a spiritual asset that leads to dependence on God. *Live each day with purpose, using your gifts to serve others, and you will bring encouragement to your soul.*

Finally, I have learned the importance of perseverance. I still pray for recovery and hope for better days, but neither of these things are guaranteed. In the meantime, I have learned to keep going, and I hope this book encourages you to keep going, too. Life with chronic illness is hard. The days are long and overwhelming. I know how exhausting and discouraging it is to fall down and pick yourself up over and over again—but you don't have to do this alone. So keep going. *Don't give up.* We are all in this together.

DRAW NEAR TO GOD

DAY 1

Seen and Known by God

I will rejoice and be glad in your steadfast love, because you have seen my affliction; you have known the distress of my soul. (Ps. 31:7)

PEOPLE WHO HAVE chronic illness know what it feels like to go through life unseen. Many chronic illnesses are invisible. You experience difficult symptoms, but no one can see when you are struggling. Even if you experience outward signs of illness or use mobility devices, you may struggle to explain to doctors, family members, and friends the extent to which symptoms impact your life.

You likely hold a desire for people to understand what you are going through. If the suffering won't go away, you at least want people to see your pain and acknowledge how much life hurts. Often people show up in the first weeks and months of poor health, but when illness persists for years or decades, support begins to fade. It's hard for people to comprehend suffering that doesn't go away.

People move on. They stop asking, which means they stop knowing. They stop showing up, which means they stop seeing. You may feel forgotten and abandoned, isolated and alone. Even if you are surrounded by supportive people who do everything they can to help and understand, at the end of the day no one can know what it is like to live inside your body but you.

It can be depressing to grapple with the reality that no one fully gets your situation—but in the end this realization leads to an important, freeing truth. The only one who can fulfill our desire to be truly seen and fully known is God. In times of suffering, Psalm 31 reminds you of an important truth: God sees your affliction. He knows the distress of your soul. God sees beyond

15

what is visible on the outside. He sees all the ways illness impacts you that no one else can fully understand. He sees beyond your circumstances and into your soul. He sees your hurt and pain, your questions and grief, your sin and doubt. He sees the times you don't know how you will keep going but somehow manage to continue on.

I often have to remind myself that no one can see my pain. I can't expect people to know when my symptoms are increasing or when I am having a hard time. I can't keep people updated on my pain levels every single time they rise and fall—nor would I want to. I don't know how to put into words why I can push through certain symptoms but not others. I can't explain these things—but God doesn't need my explanations.

God knows everything; nothing is hidden from his sight (see Heb. 4:13). Maybe you can't feel God's presence or see what he is doing, but that doesn't mean he isn't there. He sees you—even when you can't see him. He knows when no one else knows. His love is steadfast and faithful, and he will never tire of sticking with you, no matter how long your illness lasts.

Reflect: What does God know about you that no one else knows? What does God see that no one else sees? What emotion do you experience when you think about the fact that God sees your affliction and knows your soul?

Reflect: In Psalm 31, the psalmist's response to God's steadfast love is one of rejoicing and gladness. How can you rejoice in the fact that God sees your affliction and knows your soul?

Act: Don't go on this journey alone. Consider asking a wise and empathetic Christian to read this devotional with you.

DAY 2

Faith in What You Cannot See

*Now faith is the assurance of things hoped for, the
conviction of things not seen. (Heb. 11:1)*

MANY PATIENTS WHO have chronic illness wait for years to
be diagnosed. This can be an immensely trying time. In addition to
experiencing troublesome symptoms of unknown origin, patients
are often disbelieved. Doctors are quick to doubt patient reports
when blood work or imaging doesn't show anything wrong. Often,
it isn't until years later that visible evidence of underlying disease
processes begins to appear.

In my case, I experienced concerning symptoms for over a
decade before receiving a diagnosis. During this time, many doctors believed that my symptoms were real, but others did not.
Most people in my life were supportive, but some thought I was
just stressed. After all, I *looked* completely healthy. Nobody could
see my symptoms or feel my pain but me.

In those years before I received a diagnosis, I often left doctors' appointments feeling defeated. How do you get doctors to
take you seriously when the physical evidence is contrary to your
experience? In frustrated moments, we wonder, "Why can't they
take me at my word? Why can't they trust me?"

It's hard to believe in what you can't see. At the same time,
visible evidence is not always an accurate indication of what is
happening. Yes, this is true of our experiences with doctors, family members, friends, and strangers. But then it hit me—it is also
true of the way we so often relate to God.

When chronic illness disrupts our lives, we sometimes think
that because we can't see evidence of God, he isn't there. We think
that because we can't feel God's presence, he's not at work. We

struggle when we read promises in Scripture that don't seem true in our lives. God says he is good, but life is filled with suffering. God says he answers prayers, but it sure doesn't seem that way. God says he loves us, but is life with chronic illness what love looks like?

Hebrews 11:1 says that "faith is the assurance of things hoped for, the conviction of things not seen." Faith gives us two things: assurance and conviction. It gives us assurance that the hopeful things we read in Scripture are true. It gives us conviction that unseen things are real. The New King James Version uses the word *evidence*: faith is "the evidence of things not seen." Faith is the evidence that enables us to take the leap between what our eyes can see and what God tells us in Scripture.

Faith is essential, because God is invisible. We can't see God, so we have to take him at his word. Perhaps there will be times when God asks us the same questions that we ask our doctors: Will you trust me? Will you take me at my word? Just because you can't see the things I tell you doesn't mean they aren't real.

Reflect: Can you believe God's promises when visible evidence in your life seems to contradict what they say? This is exactly what we want people to do for us. And isn't God so much more trustworthy than we are?

Reflect: Faith helps you to believe in what you cannot see.

Act: Ask God to help you to trust him when things don't make sense. Pray for renewed faith, that you would believe the evidence he provides in Scripture.

DAY 3

Walk with God

Enoch walked with God, and he was not, for God took him. (Gen. 5:24)

THE SHORT STORY of one man's life can be found in Genesis 5. In the middle of a genealogy that lists the men who lived between Adam and Noah, we find a man named Enoch. If you read through the whole genealogy (see vv. 3–32), you see that Enoch's name stands out from all the rest. All the other men simply lived their lives, but Enoch was different. "Enoch walked with God, and he was not, for God took him."

Are you walking with God? Sometimes illness leads people to deeper faith in God, but other times it leads people to walk away from him. When you lose everything to your illness and God doesn't answer your prayers for healing, it's easy to feel discouraged and lost. It's easy to want to give up on your faith.

Feelings like these are understandable. Suffering is hard. Many people who have chronic illness have told me that talking to God is the last thing they want to do. How can you trust someone who has allowed so much suffering to enter your life? I understand the feeling. Sometimes I get angry at God and want to push him away. Choosing to trust is not easy. But at the end of the day, a relationship with God is what helps us to experience freedom and rest when chronic illness erodes our bodies and physical capacities.

Let me explain what I mean. We discover what Enoch's walk with God looked like in the book of Hebrews. The relationship that Enoch had with God was built on faith. Because of his faith, Enoch was commended as having pleased God (see Heb. 11:5–6). God rewarded Enoch by taking him to heaven before he died—not for any great works that he accomplished but simply because Enoch sought him (see v. 6).

God doesn't want the things that you could be *doing* if you were healthy. All he wants is you. He wants your faith, not your works. He wants your company, not grand feats. He wants to get to know you, and this is something you can do no matter what your daily life with illness looks like.

As I began to write this book, I asked myself a question. What is the number one message that people with chronic illness need to hear? What is the most important lesson that my own experience has taught me? In the end, I realized it was this: Your relationship with God is vital for your survival. People will let you down. Symptoms will come and go. Life will be painful and filled with grief. God is your only certainty.

Seek God, and you will find him (see Deut. 4:29). Draw near to God, and he will draw near to you (see James 4:8). The story of Enoch teaches an important lesson. If all that you ever do, all the days of your earthly life, is to walk with God, then that is a life worth living. That is a life worthy of being recorded and remembered for generations to come.

Reflect: How has chronic illness impacted your relationship with God? Are you walking with God or away from him? What questions or doubts, if any, make it difficult for you to be in a relationship with him?

Reflect: What steps could you take this week to walk with God? How can you make your relationship with God the most important thing?

Act: Talk to a strong believer who has suffered. Ask about his or her walk with God.

DAY 4

Say How Much It Hurts

*Be gracious to me, O L*ORD*, for I am in distress; my eye is wasted from grief; my soul and my body also. For my life is spent with sorrow . . . my strength fails because of my iniquity, and my bones waste away. . . . Those who see me in the street flee from me. I have been forgotten like one who is dead; I have become like a broken vessel. (Ps. 31:9–12)*

IN PSALM 31, David tells God about his suffering and shares the details of how it has impacted all areas of his life. His body is weak and wasting away. He feels many difficult emotions, including distress, grief, and sorrow. On a spiritual level, a heavy weight of guilt and sin saps his strength. Suffering has also impacted his relationships—friends and acquaintances dread seeing him so much that when they run into him in public they turn around and head the other way.

David is in anguish, and everyone else has moved on and forgotten that he even exists. After years of sorrow, he feels like a broken vessel. He is like a pot that has been dropped on the ground, lying in shattered pieces that are waiting to be thrown away—no longer of use to anyone.

David voices many thoughts and feelings that people with chronic illness may relate to, and he doesn't avoid saying any of them out loud. As he talks to God, he puts everything on the table. What's more, it has been noted that because Psalm 31 is addressed to the chief musician, we can know that this song was written to be sung in public.[1] Through this psalm, David tells his whole community how much he is hurting, and in the process he provides words to help them describe their own similar experiences of hurt.

Too often, we equate faithfulness in suffering with silence.

21

But what if faithfulness in suffering happens through conversation? What if faithfulness in suffering happens through speaking our hurts aloud to God and to trustworthy people, just as David does in this psalm?

Don't underestimate the power of speaking your suffering out loud. I first shared the story of my chronic health problems through my writing, and it's hard to explain the level of emotional healing and relief I felt the first time I told the truth about my pain and heard other people say, "Me too." Telling my story to God and to other people is how I have grieved my losses, processed my situation, and determined my next steps forward.

When our suffering and sorrow can't be fixed, they should be brought out into the open. This is what it means to lament. A lament is an outward expression of grief and sorrow, and it is the model God gives us in Scripture for responding to pain and loss. Far from asking us to remain silent when we suffer, God shows us how to speak our hurts aloud and even provides words in Scripture for when we cannot find our own.

Reflect: Have you ever equated faithfulness in suffering with silence? If so, how can you start being faithful in suffering through conversation? What have you avoided saying out loud?

Act: Speak the uncensored truth about your illness to God. Tell him how it impacts each area of life that David mentions in this psalm: body, soul, emotions, and relationships.

DAY 5

Trust the Lord

*Trust in the LORD with all your heart, and do not lean on
your own understanding. In all your ways acknowledge him,
and he will make straight your paths. (Prov. 3:5–6)*

CORRIE TEN BOOM was a Dutch Christian who helped to
save many Jews during the Holocaust and was eventually caught
and detained in concentration camps for her actions. In her book
The Hiding Place, she recounts her experience of being imprisoned
along with her sister Betsie. Hungry, overworked, and abused,
Corrie and her sister eventually heard rumors of an impending
release. Corrie felt a surge of hope, but Betsie appeared unaffected. As Corrie observed her sister, she sensed that Betsie
would have been just as content serving God in prison as she had
been serving God at home.[1]

Together, Corrie and Betsie gathered with women in the concentration camp barracks to study Scripture and pray. At home,
Betsie had served food to the poor; in prison, she shared God's
Word with women who had never heard it before. The setting
and mode of service were different, but to Betsie, it didn't seem
to matter. Her only concern was to do God's work wherever he
placed her. Betsie's response made no sense to Corrie—and if I
am honest, it makes no sense to me. How could Betsie respond to
unspeakable suffering with so much peace?

I think that Proverbs 3:5–6 might be part of the answer. Betsie trusted the Lord with her whole heart. She didn't lean on her
own understanding of the world. Because she acknowledged God
in her situation, she saw life from a broadened perspective, which
enabled her to submit to his will. Her mission was to serve God,
and this didn't change based on her setting. She allowed God to

lead her down his definition of a straight path, and this resulted in her life impacting hundreds of women.

Chronic illness becomes much more difficult when we lean on our own understanding of the way that life is "supposed" to be. I know that my life didn't turn out like I thought it would, and my guess is that yours didn't either. Many people imagine that life should include a prestigious career, an active family life, their favorite leisure activities, and impressive ways of doing ministry. Illness was never part of the plan. What went wrong?

Is it possible that nothing went wrong? Is it possible that you are leaning on your own understanding? Is it possible that God is asking you to trust him? In the moment, our suffering feels like the most important part of our life story—but God is orchestrating something far bigger than our individual lives, and remembering this helps us to surrender to his will.

When we acknowledge God, he promises to make our paths straight. Straight paths don't mean freedom from suffering or the outcome we desire. God uses straight paths to lead you toward his will and his desires. He does have a plan for your life. Can you trust him to lead you where he deems right?

Reflect: In what ways might you be leaning on your own understanding today? Are you willing to trust God with "all your heart" and to acknowledge him "in all your ways"?

Reflect: Chronic illness probably came as a surprise to you. It may have changed your life plans. But it did not change God's plans or surprise him in any way. How can this comfort you?

DAY 6

Look for God in Lonely Places

But Jesus often withdrew to lonely places and prayed. (Luke 5:16 NIV)

IT'S EASY TO talk about Christian community as though it's a given in the lives of all believers. Many people think that everyone has the ability to find community if they try hard enough—and in a world that was not impacted by sin, this would be true. However, in this fallen world, it is more accurate to think of community as a "gift of grace."[1] Not everyone is privileged to experience full community all of the time.

Chronic illness can be a lonely experience. Sometimes physical limitations lead to forced periods of isolation. Some people find themselves bedbound or homebound. Other people find that they don't have energy for social connection after completing the daily tasks of life. This is often the case for me. I recently had several months of improved health and increased ability to be around people, and the contrast hit me hard. Life is so much more difficult and less fulfilling when it is lived alone.

I'm not sure we will find sufficient answers to this problem before we reach heaven, but when we experience times of loneliness, I do know that we are in good company. In Luke 5:16 we find that Jesus "often withdrew to lonely places and prayed" (NIV). The ESV says that he withdrew to places that were "desolate." It was Jesus's habit to find lonely and desolate places when he wanted to spend focused time praying to God.

Picture for a moment what these places might have been like. The word *desolate* does not bring to mind beautiful scenery. The places where he went sound depressing and uncomfortable. Based on the wording of Luke 5:16, it seems likely they were barren places in the desert wilderness.[2]

Jesus chose to go to lonely places such as these in order to escape the crowds of people who followed him, to rest after times of ministry, and most importantly to connect with God. For people who are living with chronic illness, times of isolation are often less of a choice and more of a forced necessity; but as difficult as this can be, there is meaning and purpose in these times. Often, forced periods of isolation do for us what we are not willing to do for ourselves—create room in our lives for God. For me, times of loneliness have been times of preparation and spiritual formation. I have not enjoyed these seasons, but I cannot deny how God has used them.

Pray for community. Look for creative solutions. Ask people to visit if you are able to receive them, and use precious strength to socialize. But, in times of isolation and loneliness, look for God. Remind yourself that your Savior, who lived a perfect life, purposefully sought out lonely and desolate places, because this is where he wanted to be when he prayed to his Father.

Reflect: Do you struggle with isolation or loneliness due to your chronic illness? In what ways have these times been hard on you? In what ways have they benefited you?

Act: Look for God in lonely places. During periods of isolation, spend time in prayer. Take a moment right now to write out a plan for what intentional prayer could look like in your life over the next few weeks.

Act: If you struggle to pray, ask a wise Christian friend for help and accountability. Maybe start by taking time to pray together.

DAY 7

When You Don't Know How to Pray

The Spirit helps us in our weakness. For we do not know what to pray for as we ought, but the Spirit himself intercedes for us with groanings too deep for words. And he who searches hearts knows what is the mind of the Spirit, because the Spirit intercedes for the saints according to the will of God. (Rom. 8:26–27)

SHE SAT IN my counseling office defeated. Tears streamed down her face. For the past ten years, she had suffered through severe fatigue, pain, and weakness due to a rare autoimmune disease. A strong Christian who had always had a close relationship with God, she described the sorrow she felt over how difficult it had become to pray.

As is the case with many people who have chronic illness, her symptoms were not only physical but cognitive. These cognitive symptoms had recently worsened, and she was unable to concentrate for extended periods of time. The long conversations she'd used to have with God had turned into incoherent cries for help. Did God hear her when she did not know what to say?

Prayer can be difficult when you have chronic illness. Maybe you feel overwhelmed by pain, discomfort, or fatigue. You may experience confusion, memory loss, or a lack of mental focus. Maybe you feel weighed down by depression, anxiety, or anger. Or perhaps you no longer know what to pray for. Should you pray for healing or improvement? Would it be better to pray for strength? It's hard to pray for things that feel impossible.

No matter the reason that prayer feels difficult, God provides words of comfort. He is not surprised when you struggle to pray. He knew that his people would face times of weakness, and he planned for this in advance by providing his Holy Spirit to help us. God's Spirit intercedes for you when you don't know how to pray. When you struggle to form words, when physical pain blurs your thinking, when mental fog sets in and you don't even know what you need, the Spirit intercedes for you according to the will of God. And God knows the mind of the Spirit.

While different interpretations of this verse exist, many commentators, including the preacher Charles Spurgeon, believe that the "groanings too deep for words" refer to your inarticulate cries for help when you are unable to form words.[1] God can respond to wordless prayers, because he already knows what is in your heart and already knows what you need.

Be comforted. God does not need long or complicated prayers. When your suffering is so great that all you can do is groan, even then the Spirit intercedes for you and God hears you.

Reflect: What aspects of chronic illness have made prayer hard for you? What would it look like for you to rest in Romans 8:26–27 when you don't know how to pray? How might believing this passage change the way that you feel in moments of weakness?

Act: Identify a short, one-sentence prayer based on Scripture that you can turn to in moments of weakness. Choose from the ones below, or come up with our own.

- "Be strong, and let your heart take courage; wait for the Lord!" (Ps. 27:14)
- "When I am afraid, I put my trust in you." (Ps. 56:3)
- "Lord, save me." (Matt. 14:30)
- "Jesus, Master, have mercy on [me]." (Luke 17:13)
- "Not my will, but yours, be done." (Luke 22:42)

DAY 8

A Radical Approach to Loss

Indeed, I count everything as loss because of the surpassing worth of knowing Christ Jesus my Lord. For his sake I have suffered the loss of all things and count them as rubbish, in order that I may gain Christ and be found in him, not having a righteousness of my own that comes from the law, but that which comes through faith in Christ (Phil. 3:8–9)

AS A MISSIONARY to the Gentiles, Paul often encountered Jewish leaders who believed that Gentiles needed to be circumcised in order to be right with God. In the verses that precede today's passage, Paul tells the Philippians to be on guard against this false belief. They shouldn't put their hope in works of the law such as circumcision (see Phil. 3:2–3).

Before he became a Christian, Paul fell into this same trap. He put his hope in his pedigree and his right actions, believing that these works made him righteous before God. Paul was circumcised, a direct descendent of Israel, and from the distinguished tribe of Benjamin (see Phil. 3:5). He was an elite religious leader and prided himself on keeping God's law (see v. 6). He placed his confidence in this impressive résumé. But after his conversion, he saw his works as rubbish because they had led him to believe he could gain his own righteousness. His works came between him and Christ, and he had to give them up in order to fully rest in a righteousness that was imparted through faith.

Many people who have chronic illness have a similar story. When you have a healthy body, it's easy to put your hope in the wrong places. Before illness, your own résumé may have included any number of impressive works. You were productive and capable, well-respected and influential. You worked hard and felt pride in your well-adjusted family. You were happier, more even-tempered, and more interesting. You did a lot of great things, and in one sense you did them for the Lord. But in another sense, these things came between you and God, because deep down inside you felt like you needed them in order to please him.

Chronic illness has brought many losses. You now stand before God naked—stripped of qualities and achievements that once helped you to feel capable and worthy. What have you lost? Your work or ministry? Your physical abilities and feelings of competence? Your lightheartedness and humor?

When you have nothing to offer—no works of the flesh between you and God—you more fully experience the truth that righteousness from God depends on faith. A healthy body can't save you. Productivity in work and relationships won't help you to gain Christ. Having it all together doesn't earn God's favor.

Paul teaches a radical approach to loss. Our losses are real and hard and should be mourned—but sometimes loss leads to gain. Sometimes loss leads to knowing Christ, sharing in his suffering, and attaining the resurrection of the dead (see Phil 3:10–11). Sometimes loss shows us we were putting hope in ourselves without even realizing it.

Reflect: What things in life have you used as a buffer between you and God to make yourself more pleasing to him? Did you lose any of these things to illness, and if so, how did this impact you? In what ways, if any, has losing these things allowed you to gain Christ?

Act: Meditate on the surpassing value of knowing Christ Jesus as Lord. How does that help you with your loss?

DAY 9

An Opportunity to Seek God

*In the thirty-ninth year of his reign Asa was diseased in his feet,
and his disease became severe. Yet even in his disease he did not seek
the LORD, but sought help from physicians. (2 Chron. 16:12)*

KING ASA, the third king of Judah, begins his reign as a godly
man who ushers in a great revival. He tears down idols, seeks
God's help in times of war, offers sacrifices, and establishes a new
covenant between Judah and the Lord.

For thirty-five years of his reign, Asa remains faithful. Then,
for unknown reasons, he breaks the oath he has made with God
to seek him with all his heart and soul. When conflict breaks
out between King Asa and the northern kingdom of Israel, Asa
fails to go to God for help. Instead, he takes treasure from God's
house and uses it to bribe King Ben-Hadad of Syria to come to
his aid.

Asa's plan is successful at first. King Ben-Hadad helps him
to gain dominance over Israel. But then the plan backfires. Asa
receives a message from the Lord: "Because you relied on the
king of Syria, and did not rely on the LORD your God, the army of
the king of Syria has escaped you" (2 Chron. 16:7). Asa has made
a huge error. He has failed to realize that Syria is his enemy, and
after years of rest, Judah now faces a conflict that will continue for
generations to come. Angered at this news, Asa turns away from
God and begins to brutally oppress his people.

After these events, we learn only one more thing about
Asa before he dies. He becomes afflicted with a severe disease
in his feet—"yet even in his disease he did not seek the LORD,
but sought help from physicians" (2 Chron. 16:12). Just as Asa
sought help from King Ben-Hadad instead of from God in a time

of war, in the same way he seeks help from physicians instead of from God in a time of ill health.

King Asa was right to seek physicians, but he was wrong to seek *only* physicians. He was wrong to favor his body to the neglect of his soul. We should not assume that Asa would have been healed if he had sought God. Neither should we assume that God struck Asa with illness in order to teach him a lesson, or that the disease was a consequence for Asa's sin. What does seem clear is that Asa missed an opportunity to break his pattern of relying on men instead of on God.

Illness could have reminded Asa of his weakness and mortality. It could have reminded him of his utter need for God in this life and in the next. It could have reminded him of the covenant that he once held in such high importance and compelled him to return to the love that he had at first (see Rev. 2:4). If only he had been paying attention.

Illness isn't a blessing. It also isn't a punishment. Many times, it *can* serve as a reminder for us to repent and an opportunity for us to turn back to God. Illness can remind us to pray. Prompt us to turn from sin. Reveal misplaced priorities. Create space for us to repair relationships. Clarify worthier life goals. Are we paying attention?

Reflect: In your search for a diagnosis, relief, or a cure, have you forgotten to seek the Lord? Like Asa, have you relied only on physicians?

Reflect: Is God using illness to get your attention? Is he using it to remind you of something important?

Act: Ask the Lord to help you to rely on him instead of on men.

TAKE CARE OF
YOURSELF

DAY 10

Take Care of Your Body

The body is ... [meant] for the Lord, and the Lord for the body. And God raised the Lord and will also raise us up by his power.... Or do you not know that your body is a temple of the Holy Spirit within you, whom you have from God? You are not your own, for you were bought with a price. So glorify God in your body. (1 Cor. 6:13–14, 19–20)

HOW YOU VIEW your body impacts how you treat your body. The church in Corinth is an example of this. They elevated the soul and devalued the body, which led them to believe that they could use their bodies however they wanted. In response, Paul taught them some important truths about the physical bodies that God gives us.

Your body is meant for the Lord (v. 13). Paul explained to the Corinthians that their bodies were not meant for sexual immorality but were meant for God. Our bodies should be used not for sin but for God's good purposes.

Your body's final destination is resurrection and glorification (v. 14). Your body won't be discarded when you die. God will "transform our lowly body to be like his glorious body" (Phil. 3:21). One day your body will be raised up and will exist in the new heavens and the new earth. How you treat your body should reflect its final destination.[1]

Your body is the temple of the Holy Spirit (v. 19). Your body is holy (see 1 Cor. 3:17). What if you treated your body with the same respect and appreciation that you reserve for holy places?

Your body is not your own—God paid a price for your body, and it belongs to him (v. 19–20). Keep watch over your body, attending to it and guarding it carefully, for it belongs to God.

God calls you to glorify him in your body (v. 20). Two ways you can do this are by living for him in everything (see 1 Cor. 10:31) and by serving him and his people (see 1 Peter 4:10–11). When you prioritize the health and wellness of your body, you maximize your ability to glorify God in these ways.

When you have a chronic illness, the time that you spend caring for your body can feel meaningless. Days that are focused on personal self-care can feel selfish or lead to guilt. But these verses show that God holds your body in the highest regard. God approves when you put great effort into caring for your body. He approves of the dozens of doctors' appointments. The time-consuming diets and complicated treatments. The days of rest and focused self-care. Take care of your body, with the confidence that each of your efforts glorifies God.

Reflect: How do you treat things that were made for an important purpose? How do you treat things that are headed to glorious places? How do you treat things that belong to someone who sacrificed everything for you? How do you treat spaces where important people live? Your answers to these questions are a good indication of how you should treat your body.

Reflect: Do you ever neglect physical self-care in a way that makes it more difficult for you to glorify God in your body? If so, how can you begin treating your body in a way that will maximize your ability to glorify God through the ways that you live and serve?

DAY 11

God Is Practical about
Physical Needs

[Elijah] asked that he might die, saying, "It is enough; now, O LORD, take away my life. . . ." And he lay down and slept. . . . And behold, an angel touched him and said to him, "Arise and eat." And he looked, and behold, there was at his head a cake baked on hot stones and a jar of water. And he ate and drank and lay down again. (1 Kings 19:4–6)

ELIJAH IS ON the run. He has just slaughtered the prophets of Baal and has shown a great crowd of people that God is the Lord—and that Baal is not (1 Kings 18). He has incited the rage of Ahab and Jezebel, who have vowed to take his life. Terrified, he runs into the wilderness, and a day into his journey he feels unable to continue. He sits under a tree and prays for death. He calls out to God, "It is enough; now, O LORD, take away my life."

Imagine how he must feel. In order to wish for death, he probably feels hopeless and despairing. We can imagine that, after traveling for a whole day, he feels weak and fatigued as well. He also seems to be in a spiritually fragile place. His suffering is so great that he doesn't have the spiritual resources to believe that God will provide him with a way out other than death.

Notice how God responds to Elijah's cry for help. He doesn't reprimand Elijah for wishing to die. He doesn't rebuke him for not having strong enough faith or suggest that he push through his physical limitations. Later in the story, he does work through Elijah's wilderness wanderings for his spiritual good (see 1 Kings 19:9–14). But in this moment of crisis, God does not insist that Elijah learn a spiritual lesson or use his suffering for sanctification and growth. Instead, he responds to Elijah's physical and spiritual weakness by focusing on his physical needs. God leads him to a tree where he falls asleep. An angel appears and gives him food and water—not once, but twice (see 1 Kings 19:7).

God is practical about physical needs. When you feel beat down and discouraged, when you have had enough and want to give up, when your suffering feels so great that you want to die—call out to God for help, as Elijah did. But don't over-spiritualize your situation. Sometimes what you need most is a nap, a snack, and a glass of water.

Once Elijah ate, drank, and slept, his life became clearer. He continued his journey and went on to have a powerful encounter with God (see 1 Kings 19:9–18). It's interesting to consider that he wouldn't have had the physical capacity to continue his journey and meet God if he hadn't stopped and taken care of his body.

Reflect: Do you ever forget to engage in basic physical self-care? What types of self-care are you most prone to forget? When you forget to take care of your body, how does this impact your emotional and spiritual state?

Act: God is practical about physical needs, and you should be too. Stay nourished and hydrated as you are able. Do what you can to get adequate sleep. Take your medications. Stay active if you can. Rest instead of pushing through.

Act: Some people who have chronic illness experience suicidal thoughts. If you become preoccupied with thoughts of death, reach out to a trusted friend or find a counselor. If your thoughts ever intensify into a plan or you intend to kill yourself, call 911 or go to the nearest emergency room.

DAY 12

Care for Yourself in Community

Bear one another's burdens, and so fulfill the law of Christ.
For if anyone thinks he is something, when he is nothing, he
deceives himself. But let each one test his own work, and then his
reason to boast will be in himself alone and not in his neighbor.
For each will have to bear his own load. (Gal. 6:2–5)

DO YOU EVER feel like a burden? I personally find it hard to watch people taking up my slack when illness prevents me from completing certain tasks. Fortunately, Galatians 6 helps me. In this passage, we find that God designed us to live in an interdependent community in which each member gives help, receives help, and takes responsibility for his or her own load. Living in light of this passage helps us to find the humility to accept the help we need and also protects those who care for us from burnout.

Scripture tells us to bear one another's burdens, which carries the implication that we will sometimes be on the receiving end. If you struggle to accept help in this way, you are not alone. I don't like asking for help, and Galatians highlights one reason why. I deceive myself into thinking I am something when I am nothing. In other words, I struggle to see myself accurately from a humble perspective. Can you relate? It's easy to think that we should have it all together; when, in reality, Scripture repeatedly recognizes our weakness and our need for others.

This problem of pride is also one reason why we struggle to help bear the burdens of others. When illness allows us to help in only small ways, sometimes it doesn't seem like enough, and it can feel easier to for us do nothing. This is an understandable feeling, but we shouldn't underestimate our abilities. It is our responsibility to do the tasks we can, even if those tasks are easier for someone else. It is our responsibility to stay watchful of our caregivers and make sure that they don't burn out. It is our privilege to offer a listening ear and to share encouraging words when that is all we have to give.

The final instruction in this passage is for us to carry our own load. The difference between a burden and a load has to do with heaviness—a burden is something of great weight, while a load is more generally something that needs to be carried.[1] While there are many heavy aspects of illness that we need help with, in the end, no one can do the daily work of illness for us.

Living in light of this passage takes all the guilt and shame out of needing help. I can't do this alone. Neither can you. We all need each other.

Reflect: How do you let pride get in the way of asking for help? How do you let it get in the way of giving help to others?

Act: Test your own work. Write down a list of all the tasks in your life that are impacted by your illness. Include items that relate to caring for your body, chores around the house, and other responsibilities such as work, parenting, and ministry. Divide this list into two sections—one that represents burdens you are unable to carry on your own and another that represents your own load. Make note of any discrepancies between your lists and the way you are living your life. Are you carrying burdens on your own that are too much for you? Are you handing some of your load to others when it is your responsibility? Where you find discrepancies, take action to right them.

DAY 13

Find Rest

"Come to me, all who labor and are heavy laden, and I will give you rest. Take my yoke upon you, and learn from me, for I am gentle and lowly in heart, and you will find rest for your souls. For my yoke is easy, and my burden is light." (Matt. 11:28–30)

DO YOU EVER apologize for circumstances related to your illness that are outside your control? I know I do. All the time. "I'm sorry I can't hang out." "I'm sorry the house is a disaster." "I'm sorry I can't serve that day." Just yesterday I apologized to someone that my pain has been flaring, as though my very bodily existence is something to feel sorry about.

It gets worse. Underneath these spoken apologies are the ones that I leave unsaid: "I'm sorry for being this lesser version of me." "I'm sorry for not being enough." "If I were better and stronger, illness wouldn't control my life in this way."

Take note of your apologies, because they often reveal your guilt and your shame. Guilt for the things you are unable to do, and shame for the person illness has made you to be. Many people with illness carry a heavy yoke on their shoulders, leaving them buckling under the weight of unmet expectations and unrealized things that they "ought" to do and be.

In response, Jesus says, "Come to me." Learn from me. Exchange your burden for mine. Find rest for your weary soul. When Jesus spoke these words, he likely had the legalism of the Pharisees in mind. These religious leaders appeared righteous on the outside, but their hearts were far from God (see Matt. 15:8). They placed heavy, cumbersome loads on people's shoulders by teaching them to place their hope in all the right things they were supposed to do (Matt. 23:4).

The Pharisees did not understand who Jesus was. They didn't understand what it meant to exchange the yoke of the law for the yoke of being his disciple. And often, no matter how many times we hear the gospel, we fail to understand what it means for our daily lives, too.

We are saved by grace through faith. It isn't because of anything that we do. It is a gift of God and not a result of our works (see Eph. 2:8–9). Let go of people-pleasing and self-sufficiency. Let go of self-imposed "oughts" and "shoulds." Let go of working to earn God's love.

As I have responded to this invitation in my own life, I have seen a connection between soul rest and physical rest. When your soul rests in what Jesus has done for you, the guilt you feel for all you are unable to do begins to fade. You stop your anxious laboring and start learning from Jesus and sitting at his feet (see Luke 10:38–42). You learn that God does not love you more when you do more. The work that God has for you is to believe in the One he has sent (see John 6:29). Hear the good news of Jesus and find rest for your weary soul.

> **Reflect:** Do you feel guilt or shame for all you are unable to do and be? Do you find yourself anxiously laboring for God's approval? How can you remind yourself of the freedom and rest that you can find in Jesus?
>
> **Reflect:** The salvation that Jesus brings is a gift. The proper response to a gift is to say "Thank you," not "I'm sorry." What if you started thanking God for his gift of grace instead of unnecessarily apologizing for your areas of weakness and inadequacy?

Make Unpopular Decisions

*The fear of man lays a snare, but whoever trusts
in the LORD is safe. (Prov. 29:25)*

DO YOU EVER make decisions that are harmful to your body
out of a desire to please others? You should have rested instead of
going out, but you didn't want your friends to be upset. Cleaning
the house can leave you incapacitated for weeks, but you did it so
people wouldn't think you are lazy. You were so ashamed when
people found out you take pain medications that you stopped.
Over and over again, you make decisions that aren't good for your
body so people won't get upset and you won't feel embarrassed.

The consequences of people-pleasing can be costly. As Proverbs 29:25 says, when we make decisions out of a fear of man,
we fall into dangerous traps. We overextend our bodies. We make
foolish choices. It's so easy to push through—to pretend that
everything is fine. We have reputations to uphold, after all. People
to serve. Responsibilities to meet. In reality, many of us can pretend for only so long before our bodies start falling apart.

Proverbs offers an antidote to our people-pleasing tendencies. Those moments when we want to make decisions out of fear
should lead us to refocus on trusting the Lord. When we trust
God with our reputations out of a desire to please him instead of
others, we are able to make decisions that are truly faithful. These
are so much better than decisions that merely *appear* faithful on
the outside.

Faithfully caring for our bodies often requires disappointing
people, and this is okay. At times, we need to cancel plans, say no
to requests, and choose things that our bodies need over things
that other people want. Sometimes our decisions may appear

selfish or ungodly to others. People will not understand. They will question our judgment. It is painful for us to realize that we can't live up to other people's expectations. But it is also very freeing.

You may be surprised by the freedom you find to make decisions that don't make sense to people when your first priority is to honor God. This is because the Lord sees not as man sees (see 1 Sam. 16:7). He sees your heart when people cannot. God doesn't judge your decisions based on how they look on the outside. He looks at your motives, desires, and intentions. Because of this, many decisions that other people question make perfect sense to God.

It's okay to make unpopular decisions. Sometimes they are the wise choice. You are the only person who knows what your body can tolerate. You are the only one who knows how a decision will impact you and numerous other people into the future. You may be the only person who understands that putting your body first in the short run is how you put other people first in the long run. But God understands, too. He understands your reasoning, because he knows your heart. Let this make all the difference in your daily choices.

Reflect: When you have to make difficult decisions that other people may not understand, ask yourself a few questions. Am I tempted to make this decision out of people-pleasing tendencies, outside pressure, or guilt? What are my intensions and motivations as I make this decision? How can I trust the Lord as I make the decision?

Act: Write down one unpopular decision that you know you need to make. After asking God for wisdom, carry out your decision boldly.

A Spiritual Struggle

Be strong in the Lord. . . . Put on the whole armor of God, that you
may be able to stand against the schemes of the devil. For we do not
wrestle against flesh and blood, but against the rulers, against the
authorities, against the cosmic powers over this present darkness, against
the spiritual forces of evil in the heavenly places. (Eph. 6:10–12)

PEOPLE SAY OFFENSIVE things about chronic illness. It's not uncommon for people to make our illness about themselves and about how it inconveniences them. Other people assume that we would get better if we tried harder and subtly shame us for not trying treatments that they think would heal us. It's frustrating when people compare their broken leg to our chronic symptoms. It's hurtful when they seem unaffected by our suffering or choose not to accommodate our needs.

When these offenses are malicious or abusive, they require careful measures that ensure physical and emotional safety.[1] But even in ordinary circumstances, it's hard for us to know what to do—especially when close and important relationships are involved. Should we be up-front and honest about our hurt and speak the truth in love (see Eph. 4:15)? Should we let it go and allow love to cover a multitude of sins (see 1 Peter 4:8)? When people say hurtful things to us, how do we stop bitterness and anger from growing in our hearts?

Over the years, I have realized how much Satan loves division. He wants us to believe that our suffering is special and that no one could understand what we are going through. He wants us to believe that the people who offend us have perfect lives and no problems. He wants us to believe that people are cruel, when often they are merely uneducated. He wants us to think that relationships are impossible, when many times they could be repaired with forgiveness and honest communication.

It's so easy to forget that we are on the same side. We do not fight against flesh and blood. Chronic illness is not our biggest problem, and the people who misunderstand us are not our enemies. Scripture does not deny that problematic people exist. But, too often, these relational struggles and misunderstandings distract us from the spiritual battle that wages around us.

Your true battle is against rulers, authorities, cosmic powers over this present darkness, and spiritual forces of evil in heavenly places. Constantly feeling offended by people who misunderstand our illnesses doesn't win spiritual battles. In fact, it does the opposite. It pits us against one another, when something much bigger is at stake.

We stand against the schemes of the devil by putting on the armor of God and fighting this spiritual battle together. Together we seek truth, righteousness, and faith. Together we seek the gospel and salvation, focus on God's Word, and pray at all times in the Spirit. None of us can win this battle alone.

Reflect: Has chronic illness led you to struggle against people in your life? If so, how have these struggles distracted you from the more important spiritual struggle that we all wrestle against together?

Reflect: Proverbs 19:11 says, "Good sense makes one slow to anger, and it is his glory to overlook an offense." How can you be slow to anger this week? What offenses might God be asking you to overlook this week?

Reflect: In order to thrive spiritually, we need each other. Consider Proverbs 17:17; Ephesians 4:15–16; Hebrews 3:12–13; 10:24–25.

DAY 16

One Day at a Time

"Do not be anxious about tomorrow, for tomorrow will be anxious for itself. Sufficient for the day is its own trouble." (Matt. 6:34)

MANY PEOPLE WHO have chronic illness struggle with some level of worry. This has been the case for me. Before I was diagnosed, it was terrifying to know that my body was deteriorating without knowing why. Once I received a name for my illness, some of these fears began to dissipate, but other worries lingered.

Will my symptoms get worse? Will this pain last forever? Will my body be able to manage my plans for tomorrow, or will I need to cancel? When I worry, it's not usually about whether I can handle the pain of the present moment. Foremost on my mind during times of anxiety is how long I can handle not having any relief and whether relief will ever come.

Your worries may be different from mine, but likely they take you into the future. Maybe you experience anxiety about eating or sleeping. You may worry about traveling or being isolated and alone. You may worry about what your symptoms mean, how serious they are, or whether treatments will work. Will you ever feel better? How will you keep going day after day?

Life with chronic illness is filled with things to worry about, and this can make Jesus's words in Matthew 6:34 feel frustrating. In theory, we understand the wisdom in Jesus's instructions. We know we can't predict all of tomorrow's problems or fix them preemptively. We understand that we have only enough bandwidth to take care of today's issues and that we should focus on the present as a result. This wisdom sounds great in theory, but it can feel impossible to practice.

Here is something that has helped me to live out this verse.

In times of worry, I ask myself a few questions. The first question is "Can I endure the pain of this present moment?" This question helps me to stop worrying about tomorrow by reminding me that I have to face only one moment at a time.

The second question is "What do I need right now, and are there any practical steps I can take to meet this need?" When Jesus says, "Sufficient for the day is its own trouble," his implication seems to be that we should focus on managing the troubles of the present day. This question helps me to follow through on needed action.

The final question is "Do I believe that God cares for me?" Earlier in Matthew 6, Jesus reminds us that we have a Father who sees us as valuable (see v. 26) and who knows what we need (see v. 32). In times of worry, it's easy for us to forget about God. It's easy to forget that he is present and actively working in our lives and that he cares about the things we fear. This question reminds me to cast my cares on God, in the knowledge that he will sustain me (see Ps. 55:22).

Reflect: Do you struggle with worry? If so, what do you worry about? How many of your worries are based in the future? When you are able to focus on the present day, how does this impact your worries?

Act: Write these three questions down on a notecard, and read them each time you feel anxious: Can I endure the pain of this present moment? What do I need right now and are there any practical steps I can take to meet this need? Do I believe that God cares for me?

DAY 17

Chronic Illness and Your Thoughts

Finally, brothers, whatever is true, whatever is honorable,
whatever is just, whatever is pure, whatever is lovely, whatever
is commendable, if there is any excellence, if there is anything
worthy of praise, think about these things. (Phil. 4:8)

I HAVE A friend who likes to ask me two questions: "How are you feeling?" and "How are you thinking?" She is a wise friend who also has chronic illness. She knows that my body always feels some level of distress but that, in the end, my thinking determines how I'm really doing that day. When my thinking is in a good place, I can better handle whatever my body throws at me. When my thoughts go to dark or fearful places, my physical symptoms are much more difficult.

How are you thinking today? It's easy to ruminate on symptoms and limitations that feel unfair. It's easy to dwell on difficult circumstances and to pine for a different life. It's easy to feed negative thoughts, which lead to negative emotions, which make all of life seem dark and hopeless.

We shouldn't suppress difficult thoughts. We need to grieve the losses of illness, and this involves processing hard thoughts, not ignoring them or immediately trying to replace them. At the same time, it's easy for us to indulge in thought patterns that are sinful or that make life more difficult. In such times, the book of Philippians offers practical advice.

The content of our thoughts matters. Our thinking should focus on things that are true, honorable, just, pure, lovely, commendable, excellent, and praiseworthy. When Paul says that we should think about these things, he isn't referring to passing thoughts. Paul is telling us to consider, take into account, weigh, or meditate on thoughts that meet these criteria.[1] This type of thinking takes time, and it doesn't happen automatically.

It takes pointed effort to meditate on certain thoughts. We have to become aware of those times when our thinking drifts to unhelpful places, identify other thoughts that will meet Paul's criteria, and find the willpower to move from one to the other. All this can sound like instructions for positive thinking, but I don't think that's what this passage is suggesting.

Note that the first word in Paul's list is *true*. Paul isn't suggesting that we turn our thinking from negative to positive. He's redirecting our thoughts from lies to truth—and the best place for us to find true thoughts is in Scripture. Rather than reading true thoughts in Scripture and then forgetting them, we should find true thoughts and keep them in mind. I wonder how our mindset and general well-being might change if we made a point to do this every day.

Reflect: How are you thinking today? How is your thinking impacting your emotions and general outlook on life? How is it impacting your actions? Are you thinking true thoughts today? Are your thoughts honorable, just, pure, lovely, commendable, excellent, and praiseworthy?

Act: Find a true thought in Scripture, memorize it, and meditate on it throughout the day. Note how it impacts your thinking, feeling, and general outlook on life. If you struggle to find one of your own, consider these:

- "God is our refuge and strength, a very present help in trouble." (Ps. 46:1)
- "Blessed are those who mourn, for they shall be comforted." (Matt. 5:4)
- "Jesus Christ is the same yesterday and today and forever." (Heb. 13:8)

DAY 18

Wisdom for Unpredictable Days

When times are good, be happy; but when times are bad, consider this: God has made the one as well as the other. Therefore, no one can discover anything about their future. (Eccl. 7:14 NIV)

CHRONIC ILLNESS IS unpredictable. You never know how you will feel from day to day or from hour to hour. One day you wake up feeling decent, and the next day you feel like you have been hit by a truck. The reason for the sudden change is uncertain. The ups and downs are erratic and exhausting. You work hard to figure out what triggers your symptoms, but if you are like many people, this may feel like a fruitless effort. Your body does what it wants, when it wants, just because it wants to.

It is demoralizing to never know how your body will feel or respond. Something that causes symptoms one day may be just what your body needs in order to feel better the next. Will it be a good pain day or a bad pain day? Will new symptoms stay indefinitely or leave in a few hours? Will you be able to follow through with your schedule tomorrow, or will you have to cancel? Life is filled with uncertainty, and nothing feels in your control.

We find a straightforward description of life's unpredictability in Ecclesiastes 7:14. Life includes good days. It also includes bad days. You never know which type of day tomorrow will be, because you can't see into the future. This is true for everyone, but chronic illness brings this fact into the spotlight.

How should we respond to this roller coaster of good and bad days? By taking each day as it comes. When you have a good day, live in the moment. Be happy! God gave you that day. Don't waste it wondering what tomorrow will be like, because it's impossible for you to know. Only God knows your future.

Bad days come out of the blue. Flares and crashes, setbacks and increased symptoms. It feels discouraging and unfair, and it's easy to want to give up. On days like these, Ecclesiastes says to stop and call God to mind. Remember that God is sovereign over all your days—both good and bad.

It can be upsetting to consider this truth. It means that God could take away your bad days but chooses not to. I'm not always sure what to do with this fact. Bad days of symptoms feel purposeless, and Ecclesiastes doesn't give a reason for bad times. It is simply honest about the fact that bad days exist and encourages us to turn our thoughts toward God when they happen.

Considering God on bad days is an act of faith and trust. Life is unpredictable, but Jesus is the same yesterday, today, and forever (see Heb. 13:8). Suffering often doesn't make sense, but God is trustworthy all the same. At the end of the day, God questions us and we answer to him—not the other way around (see Job 38:3)—because he is the Creator and Sustainer of all things.

> **Reflect:** How do you normally respond to good days? Can you be happy on good days? Can you take advantage of the God-given gift of a good day? What is one way you can celebrate the next time you have a good day?
>
> **Reflect:** How do you normally respond to bad days? Can you consider God on bad days? What is one way you can consider God the next time you have a bad day?

DAY 19

Look for Jesus When
You Feel Ashamed

*Those who look to him are radiant, and their faces
shall never be ashamed. (Ps. 34:5)*

I OFTEN SIT down in church during praise and worship due to
chronic pain. The worship leader calls everyone to stand, and I do
for a while. Then, depending on how I feel that day, I tend to sit
down sometime between the end of the first song and the beginning of the last. Sitting down while everybody else stands makes
me feel like a sore thumb. What are people thinking about me?
Do they think I am disrespectful? Lazy? Uninterested?

Sometimes I feel people look at me, and I start to feel embarrassed and ashamed. One Sunday I heard the child behind me
whisper to his mother, "Mommy, why is she sitting down? Aren't
we supposed to be standing?" Moments like this remind me that
I am different. My body is broken, and people around me notice.

This feeling of shame has sometimes distracted me from the
service, but as I sat down one Sunday, it hit me that it is impossible for me to feel ashamed and to worship at the same time. It is
impossible for me to sing words of praise to God and simultane-
ously feel embarrassed. When I look directly at Jesus, when my
eyes are on him, there is no room for shame to grow in my heart.
I don't care what people think. I care only about the focus of my
attention.

David explains this experience when he writes, "Those who
look to him are radiant, and their faces shall never be ashamed."
David was a man on the run—being hunted down by King Saul.
In his distress, he looked to the Lord. What about us? When we

look to Jesus, we can't also fully focus on our shame. But when we're distracted by shame, we struggle to engage with our Savior.

Whether because of embarrassing symptoms, the need for accommodations, or the feeling of being "other," many people who have chronic illness experience feelings of shame on a regular basis. In those moments, Psalm 34:5 teaches you how to turn your gaze away from the stares of others and from your own judgmental thoughts and to look at Jesus.

We can live out this verse in a variety of ways. Sometimes it looks like worshiping Jesus in moments of shame, as I did. Other times it looks like serving him or praying to him in moments of shame. You may learn to care about his opinions and set your mind on his thoughts instead of on the stares of others. Instead of being pulled inward, toward your shame, look outward toward Christ and engage with him.

When you look to him in these ways, Jesus not only takes away your shame but also changes your countenance. In the light of his glory, you radiate who he is to those around you. As you serve, worship, pray, and draw your thoughts toward Christ, you reflect who he is for all to see.

Reflect: Do you experience shame related to your chronic illness? If so, what specific aspects of your illness feel most shameful? How do you respond when you feel ashamed? Do you hide? Avoid certain people and places? Shut down? Struggle to engage with Christ or the people around you?

Act: Write out a list of all the times you felt ashamed about your chronic illness in the last day, week, or month. For each of those moments, think of one or two specific ways you could have turned your focus away from your shame and toward Jesus.

DAY 20

Toil and Strive for Godliness

Train yourself for godliness; for while bodily training is of some value,
godliness is of value in every way, as it holds promise for the present
life and also for the life to come. . . . To this end we toil and strive,
because we have our hope set on the living God, who is the Savior
of all people, especially of those who believe. (1 Tim. 4:7–8, 10)

DO YOU EVER feel like God would be more pleased with you if you could do more? It's an easy thought to have. We live in a have-it-all world that prizes strength and productivity. When chronic illness saps your strength and reduces your ability to be productive, it's easy to wonder if God wants you to give more than you feel able to give.

There is nothing wrong with training our bodies to be stronger and more capable so that we can do more. Many people who have chronic illness find it essential to train their bodies every day in order to avoid deconditioning and to control various symptoms. Scripture recognizes the value in this. When our bodies are healthy, we have a better quality of life and are better able to serve our families and communities. These are both good things.

I'm thankful they are not the most important things, because physical fitness can be discouraging when you have chronic illness. Every day I do physical therapy exercises, and often all my hard work serves only to keep me from declining. I once loved bodily training, but now it is a demoralizing endeavor.

God is wise and kind. Our ability to please him doesn't rest on our physical capacity. His pleasure is not "in the legs of a man" (Ps. 147:10). His pleasure in you does not depend on your ability to stand, walk, or run. He does not love you more when you can clean the house and go to work than when you are lying in bed.

There is no physical feat you can do that will make him delight in you more than he already does.

God gives us a place to direct our efforts when we feel discouraged by our physical incapacities. This life is not a race to become physically fit and strong. It is a spiritual race that spans both this present life and the life to come. We long for physical capacity, because it holds true value in this life; but in our discouragement, God points us to something better and longer-lasting. Godliness, not increased physical strength, is the end to which we should toil and strive (see 1 Tim. 4:8, 10). Fear of God and hope in his love is what brings God pleasure (see Ps. 147:11).

Reflect: Do you ever feel like God would be more pleased with you if you could do more? If so, where do you think you learned to feel this way? Instead of toiling and striving for physical fitness or greater strength, what would it look like for you to toil and strive for godliness?

Act: When you feel discouraged by your inability to gain physical strength, set your heart on growing in your fear of God (see Ps. 147:10–11). You can do this by seeking friendship with the Lord (see Ps. 25:14), keeping his commands (see Ps. 112:1), and pursuing wisdom and understanding (see Job 28:28; Ps. 111:10).

LIVE WITH PURPOSE

DAY 21

Stewards of God's Grace

As each has received a gift, use it to serve one another, as good
stewards of God's varied grace: whoever speaks, as one who
speaks oracles of God; whoever serves, as one who serves by the
strength that God supplies—in order that in everything God
may be glorified through Jesus Christ. (1 Peter 4:10–11)

As you draw near to God and take care of yourself, you
become equipped to give yourself to the needs of other people.
In this section, I want to show you that chronic illness does not
change your end mission. Every single believer is called to what
the Westminster Shorter Catechism calls man's chief end: "to
glorify God and enjoy him forever."[1]

In 1 Peter 4:10–11, we see a connection between serving one
another and bringing glory to God. Just like everyone else, people
who have chronic illness are called to look out for the interests of
others (see Phil. 2:4) and to love their neighbors as themselves
(see Mark 12:31).

This call can feel discouraging. We wonder why God would
ask us to serve and then reduce our capacity to do so. It seems that
we would be much more useful if we were healthy. Sometimes
our symptoms are so incapacitating that giving is the last thing
on our minds. At times, we are more concerned about how we
will continue to eat, sleep, breathe, walk, shower, and stay alive.
How does serving others fit into your life when you are barely
surviving?

Here's something interesting, though. This passage was written to persecuted Christians who had been forced out of their
homes and away from their communities because of their faith.
The whole book of 1 Peter is written to show suffering people

how to live and find hope. One of Peter's instructions to these persecuted believers is that even while they are suffering, they should continue doing good (see 1 Peter 4:19).

And the same is true for you. Even as you suffer, God has given you a gift. It may be the gift of speaking or serving, as mentioned in this passage. Or it could be a gift that Scripture refers to elsewhere, such as encouraging, giving, leading, showing mercy, or having faith (see Rom. 12:6–8; 1 Cor. 12:6–10). It is a unique gift that comes from God's varied grace, and he asks you to steward that gift by carrying out works that he has prepared in advance for you (see Eph. 2:10). God has created works for each of us that are perfect fits for our unique gifts and circumstances. What's more, he instructs us to use these gifts with the strength he has supplied to us—which seems to acknowledge and validate that we all have different capacities.

The ultimate reason for us to use these gifts is so that God will be glorified through Christ Jesus. He deserves our service, because glory and dominion belong to him. But God has also provided a gracious side effect of these gifts. When we use our gifts to the glory of God, we are blessed and refreshed (see Prov. 11:25). We are drawn out of our self-pity and shame. We find hope and purpose. By giving to others, we glorify God and become better equipped to face the difficult days that come with chronic illness.

Reflect: You are a steward of God's varied grace. How has this varied grace manifested itself in your life? What gift has he given you?

Act: Once you identify your gift, think of how you can use that gift with the specific amount of strength that God has given you. Then take steps to use that gift this week.

DAY 22

Praise God for Your Body

*I praise you, for I am fearfully and wonderfully made. . . . My
frame was not hidden from you, when I was being made in secret,
intricately woven in the depths of the earth. Your eyes saw my
unformed substance; in your book were written, every one of
them, the days that were formed for me. (Ps. 139:14–16)*

WHAT WORDS COME to mind when you think about your
body? No matter who you are, this is a loaded question. Most
likely, the first word to pop into your head is not *wonderful*.
When I think about my body, I immediately think of words
like *exhausted*, *painful*, and *broken*. Unlike the author of Psalm
139, when I consider my body and how it was created, I am not
inspired to spontaneously praise God.

Chronic illness can lead to a great deal of frustration, anger,
fear, and body shame. It's upsetting to have bodies that are weak,
painful, and malfunctioning. We wish away thinning hair, blem-
ished skin, and extra pounds. If only our bodies didn't develop
embarrassing symptoms that we can't even mention. Our bodies
don't *feel* wonderful. They don't *feel* holy or good. They don't even
feel normal.

God did not give me the body I want. My guess is that he
didn't give you the body you want, either. Instead, Psalm 139
suggests, he gave us the bodies we need. God made your body
with every single day of your life in mind. He created your inward
self—your heart and mind—knowing what life had in store for
you. He knit together your tissues and bones, knowing the works
he desired from you. You were intricately made with a precise set
of strengths and weaknesses that would allow you to best live out
the days ahead of you.

God was not surprised when you were born with stretchy connective tissue, missing genes, or a confused immune system. Your diagnosis may have been a shock to you, but it was never a secret to God, because he knew everything about you before you existed. Your body may not feel like the best body for you. But only an omniscient God could know the body you would need in order for your life to best display his works and glorify him (see John 9:1–41; 11:4).

Ephesians 2:10 says that you are God's workmanship created to do good works that God prepared in advance for you. Your body is fearfully and wonderfully made—perfectly created to carry out the unique works that God designed for you. So praise God for your body. Thank him for displaying his wonderful work through you.

Reflect: What physical strengths and weaknesses has God given you? How have you seen him use your physical strengths and weaknesses to help you to carry out the works that he prepared for you?

Reflect: God designed your body with purpose. Your physical weakness may be exactly what makes you indispensable to the body of Christ (see 1 Cor. 12:22).

DAY 23

God Does the Work

The LORD said to Gideon, "The people with you are too many for me to give the Midianites into their hand, lest Israel boast over me, saying, 'My own hand has saved me.'" (Judg. 7:2)

GOD OFTEN USES weak people who have limited resources to do incredible things. This was the case when he called a man named Gideon to save Israel from the oppressive nation of Midian. When Gideon first hears God's call, he feels hesitant and doubtful. He reminds God's messenger that his clan is "the weakest in Manasseh" and that he is "the least in [his] father's house" (Judg. 6:15). Gideon has to work through some serious doubt, but he eventually relents to God's summons.

He gathers thirty-two thousand men and prepares for battle, only to hear shocking news from God. God tells Gideon that his army is too big. If he fights Midian with so many men, Israel will believe they have saved themselves through their own strength. They will boast and say, "My own hand has saved me" and overlook the fact that God won the battle for them.

To avoid any confusion, God sends the vast majority of Gideon's army home, leaving only three hundred men left to fight the massive Midianite military. By all earthly appearances, they are in trouble—but God has a purpose behind his decision. You can read the details of what happens next in Judges 7. God wakes Gideon up in the middle of the night and leads his men through some outlandish battle tactics that lead to Midian's defeat. In the end, there is no question that deliverance has come not from the hand of men but from God.

Maybe you feel like Gideon. God has asked you to do something important, but you feel hesitant and confused. You are weak, limited, and under-resourced. God has asked you to be a parent, but you feel too ill to care for your children. He has asked you to provide for your family, but you struggle to get out of bed. He has called you to ministry, but you feel too physically limited to be effective.

In situations like these, God gives you the grace and wisdom to stop, say no, and rest when circumstances allow. He also gives you inconceivable strength when life provides you no choice but to keep going. He provides unexpected strategies that you never would have conceived of on your own. He makes impossible feats possible. When you look back on times like this months or years later, you see that you did not make it through by your own hand but by the grace and strength of God.

God doesn't need you to be healthy in order to complete his plan for your life. One reason he uses weak people with limited resources is because it displays that he is the one who does the work. He is the one who saves. When people see you accomplish incredible things with little strength and no resources, they recognize something supernatural in your situation, and this gives testament to God's power.

Reflect: Is God asking you to do something that you have been avoiding because you feel too weak, limited, and under-resourced? What would it look like for you to step out in faith and in the knowledge that God is the one who saves?

Act: Step out in faith. Work through your doubt, as Gideon did, and then be obedient and faithful to God's call for your life, with the confidence that his power, not your strength, will get you through.

DAY 24

Strength in Weakness

A thorn was given me in the flesh, a messenger of Satan to harass me, to keep me from becoming conceited. Three times I pleaded with the Lord about this, that it should leave me. But he said to me, "My grace is sufficient for you, for my power is made perfect in weakness." (2 Cor. 12:7–9)

AT TIMES, I have felt confused by passages in Scripture that seem to indicate that I am still sick because of a lack of faith (such as James 5:15);[1] but then I think of the apostle Paul and his thorn in the flesh. We don't know the nature of Paul's affliction, but we do know that he repeatedly prayed for his suffering to be taken away and that God said no. Paul was a great man of God. If God would deny his petition, it seems there are times when people pray in true faith and don't receive the answer they want.

Instead of relief, God gives Paul two things. He gives him sufficient grace and perfect power—two spiritual resources that are also available to you as you face your own unanswered prayers for relief.

"My grace is sufficient for you" means that the goodness and favor of God will be enough for you as you face long-term suffering. When God doesn't take your suffering away, he will give you strength to bear it. God's grace may not feel like enough in the moment, but look back on your life. Has there ever been a day when you didn't make it through? Can you think of any way to account for this other than the grace of God? In my own life, I certainly cannot.

"My power is made perfect in weakness" means that God's power is best accomplished through your life when you are weak. For me, this is most apparent in my work as a counselor. If it weren't for my illness, I would be tempted to go into counseling sessions without preparing, without praying, without facing my own inadequacy. It would be easy for me to think I have it all together and to forget my need for God.

But then I wake up in pain and wonder how I'm going to make it to work that day. I struggle to think straight and feel anxious about how my sessions will go, and so I start to pray. Weakness reminds me to connect with God, and sometimes I am amazed at the work he does through me when I feel at my worst.

I wish it didn't take sickness to remind me to pray, but too often this is the case. Weakness is painful, but we need it—because, like Paul, we are prone to pride. God allowed Satan to bring suffering into Paul's life in order to protect him from conceit and to remind him that he couldn't face hardship or ministry responsibilities on his own. What's more, if he stopped relying on himself and looked to God, God would accomplish more in his weakness than when he felt strong.

Reflect: How have you experienced God's sufficient grace as you have lived with chronic illness? How has he given you everything you've needed on days when you didn't think you would survive?

Reflect: How do you see God's power being made perfect in weakness in your own life? What has God accomplished through your weakness? In what ways, if any, has chronic illness protected you from pride or other types of sin?

DAY 25

For the Glory of God

*Now a certain man was ill, Lazarus of Bethany, the village of Mary
and her sister Martha. . . . So the sisters sent to him, saying, "Lord,
he whom you love is ill." But when Jesus heard it he said, "This
illness does not lead to death. It is for the glory of God, so that the
Son of God may be glorified through it." (John 11:1, 3–4)*

LAZARUS WAS A man who became sick, died, and then was
raised from the dead by Jesus. We don't know much else about
him. As we read through his story in John 11, it's interesting to
note that even though Lazarus is the one who is raised from the
dead, the passage isn't really about him. It is mostly about what
Jesus does in Mary, Martha, the disciples, and other onlookers
through Lazarus.

Jesus has a plan for Lazarus's illness from the beginning.
When he receives word that Lazarus is sick, he doesn't hurry to
see him. He waits for two days, until he knows that Lazarus is
dead, and tells his disciples that this is a good thing for their sake,
because it will help them to believe (see John 11:15).

As Jesus travels to Bethany, we continue to see that Lazarus's illness is not about Lazarus. Jesus and his disciples meet up
with Martha, Mary, and others who are mourning with them,
and together they make their way to Lazarus's tomb. Once there,
Jesus asks for the stone in front of the tomb to be rolled away,
but Martha is hesitant because of the smell. Jesus responds to her,
"Did I not tell you that if you believed you would see the glory of
God?" (v. 40). People roll the stone away, Jesus calls out with a
loud voice, "Lazarus, come out," and Lazarus walks out alive.

The purpose of Lazarus's illness was "for the glory of God, so
that the Son of God may be glorified through it." His illness and

death provided a setting for Jesus's power to be displayed so that people would believe he was sent by God (see v. 42) and give him honor and praise.

It is a frightening and humbling privilege that God uses illness for his glory. He uses us in ways we would never choose for ourselves. The point of Lazarus's story is not that Jesus always heals people from illness in order to bring himself glory. The point is that Jesus creates outcomes, whatever they may be, that allow his glory to be displayed through our lives of illness.

We are often reminded that all things work together for the good of those who love God (see Rom. 8:28). We might not consider that sometimes our suffering works together for the good of someone else. Your chronic illness might not be about you. It might have more to do with what God desires to do through you, so that others might believe and Jesus might be glorified.

Reflect: Have you ever considered that your chronic illness might not be about you? Can you think of people in your life whom God might be reaching through the circumstances of your illness?

Reflect: Whether you are healed or not, whether you find improvement or not, the most important thing is for God's glory to shine through your life. In what ways may God be using your illness for his glory?

Spread the Gospel

You know it was because of a bodily ailment that I
preached the gospel to you at first. (Gal. 4:13)

THE CHURCH IN Galatia heard the good news of the gospel
for the first time because the apostle Paul experienced a bodily
ailment. We don't know what the ailment was or the details of
what happened. It appears that Paul was on a missionary journey, and this verse suggests the possibility that he was headed
somewhere other than Galatia when a physical condition caused
him to change his plans. Maybe he needed a place to stop and
recover before moving on. This much seems clear: a bodily ailment uniquely situated Paul to spread the gospel to people who
may not have heard the good news of Christ otherwise.

Is it possible that God wants to use you for similar purposes?
Illness brings us to places we wouldn't otherwise go and intro-
duces us to people we wouldn't otherwise meet. It creates a shared
experience and a point of connection that leads to encounters
that wouldn't otherwise happen. Illness upends our whole lives
and, in doing so, positions us to share God's love and good news
with unreached people.

In my conversations with people who have chronic illness,
I have been encouraged by the "chance encounters" they describe
that allow them to share Christ with the people they meet. I think
of friends who have shared the gospel with their caregivers and
medical providers. I think of people who have formed ministries
out of their illnesses and of people who can't leave their beds but
who pour themselves into others they have met online.

It's easier to face hardship when you know there is purpose
behind it. Paul faced unbelievable hardship without thinking

twice because his eyes were fixed on a clear mission and goal. His priority was not his life or his health or his personal well-being. He claimed with boldness that his aim was to "finish my course and the ministry that I received from the Lord Jesus, to testify to the gospel of the grace of God" (Acts 20:24).

Because his goal was so clear, he had the courage to travel to cities where the Holy Spirit had informed him ahead of time that he would face imprisonment and affliction (see Acts 20:23). He maintained strength through illness, torture, shipwrecks, sleeplessness, back-breaking work, and all kinds of danger, because he knew that fulfilling God's purpose for his life was more important than avoiding pain.

Throughout the course of history, the gospel has been spread through hardship. God used Paul's illness to bring him to an unreached city. He called the disciples to leave their families and homes and never look back. He used persecution to scatter the church. Even to this day, he uproots individuals and families and nations. Why wouldn't he use hardship to accomplish similar purposes through you?

Reflect: How does it encourage you to know that God uses hardships such as illness to spread his gospel? How can focusing on this purpose and task give you the strength and courage to keep going?

Act: Write down a list of ways in which your illness uniquely positions you to spread the gospel. Act on what you find.

DON'T GIVE UP

Wait for Jesus

But our citizenship is in heaven. And we eagerly await a Savior from there, the Lord Jesus Christ, who, by the power that enables him to bring everything under his control, will transform our lowly bodies so that they will be like his glorious body. (Phil. 3:20–21 NIV)

THE CONFERENCE SPEAKER was talking about seasons of suffering—my least favorite topic. She told the audience to persevere. To hold on to God's promise that trials are temporary. In this life, God gives us good times and hard times. Keep going, and your good season will come.

I was in the middle of a two-year-long flare. The pain was oppressive and unrelenting. Months of physical therapy, doctors' appointments, and various medical treatments weren't helping. My suffering did not feel seasonal. It felt permanent and unbearable. What hope did she have to offer me?

In the coming years, I would experience a break from these symptoms. They wouldn't go away, but they would become more manageable. I would move into a better season, just as the speaker said. Even so, I still struggle when people talk about *seasons* of suffering.

I have friends with illnesses that are far worse than my own. Their symptoms are progressive and intractable. Some have a condition that will worsen until they die, unless God performs a miracle. Others have not received such a harsh prognosis but still live in uncertainty for years at a time. You never know whether symptoms of chronic illness will relent or not, and each minute of suffering can feel endless. How do you find peace and hold on to hope in this situation? How do you persevere and not give up when suffering doesn't stop?

The conference speaker's answers to these questions were partially true. Good does intermingle with suffering. Sometimes impossibly difficult seasons pass in the most unexpected ways. But we can't place the full weight of our hope on healing or relief here on earth, because these things may or may not come; and, if they do, they will not last. In order for us not to give up, we need more than hopeful possibilities. We need a hope that is certain.

As Christians, we find this certain hope in a Savior—the Lord Jesus Christ. One day he will come back for us, and when he does, he will forgive all our sins *and* heal all our diseases (see Ps. 103:3). Medical care may fail us. Exercise and diets will never be enough. Despite modern technology, many of us will never improve in this lifetime, and some of us will only grow worse.

Each ache and pain in our bodies reminds us that we do not belong here. We are citizens of a heavenly city where we will one day reside in new and transformed bodies. Bodies that have been transformed from weak to glorious. From broken to free from pain. One day our bodies will be like Jesus's glorious body. "Believe in the Lord Jesus Christ, and you will be saved" (Acts 16:31)—your soul, and your body also.

Reflect: Where do you look for hope and peace when you want to give up? Do you find yourself hoping in things that are uncertain or temporary? If so, would you like to shift your focus to the certain and eternal hope of Christ?

Act: If you have not trusted Christ as your Savior, you can pray and ask the Lord for faith. Christ is the only hope that is guaranteed to persist longer than chronic illness, and it is never too late to trust him.

DAY 28

Expect God's Goodness

I would have despaired unless I had believed that I would see the goodness of the LORD in the land of the living. Wait for the LORD; be strong and let your heart take courage; yes, wait for the LORD. (Ps. 27:13–14 NASB)

WHEN CHRONIC ILLNESS lasts for years that turn into decades that turn into a lifetime, without relief, it can feel impossible to believe that God wants good things for you. Expect suffering? That makes sense. Expect God's goodness? That's harder to believe.

In Psalm 27, the author, King David, expresses his belief that he will experience God's goodness in the land of the living. In hard times, David held on to an inner assurance that his life would be more than suffering. He knew that when he died he would experience the perfect presence and goodness of the Lord, but this knowledge alone was not enough to keep him from despair. He also needed faith that God would be good to him, in some way, even while he lived.

The cynical side of me wonders if this promise is true for everyone. My mind always goes to worst-case scenarios when I read verses like this. How do you believe you will one day see God's goodness, not just in heaven but also on earth, when your husband leaves you because of your illness? When your doctor takes away the pain medications you desperately need? When you lose your insurance and won't live without it? When your kids are bitter about your pain? When physical symptoms are so intense you want to die?

If you find yourself in a situation such as this and it feels impossible to believe you will experience God's goodness, David offers a suggestion. His suggestion is to wait on God.

God has not forgotten you, and he isn't out to get you. When everything seems wrong and nothing seems right, wait. Stay strong, wait for the Lord, and see what he does. Wait for the Lord with courage and expect to see his goodness in some way. This psalm does not promise that God will give you the outcome that you want. Instead, we find in it a reminder that even though life is filled with suffering, God's goodness is present too.

The longer I experience illness, the more I am able to believe in God's goodness. God keeps showing up in unexpected ways in my life and in the lives of those I love. He usually shows up after I have waited much longer than I wanted to. He provides new treatments, unexpected remission, accurate diagnoses, and improved mobility. He provides providential parking spaces, encouraging words, kind nurses, new friends, and needed prescriptions in the final hour.

Relief from suffering is not guaranteed; yet even so, the love of God fills the earth (see Ps. 119:64). I believe that I will look upon the goodness of the Lord in the land of the living. And I believe that you will too.

Reflect: What makes waiting hard for you? Do you ever feel like God has forgotten you? Do you ever find yourself falling into the mindset that he is out to get you? How can you change your mindset to believe that you will see God's goodness, somehow and in some way, in the land of the living?

Act: Write down all the ways you have seen God's goodness in the past. Write down all the ways you can see his goodness in your life right now. Then wait on him and believe that you will continue to see his goodness in the days to come.

DAY 29

Hope in God

We were so utterly burdened beyond our strength that we despaired of life itself. . . . But that was to make us rely not on ourselves but on God who raises the dead. He delivered us from such a deadly peril, and he will deliver us. On him we have set our hope that he will deliver us again. (2 Cor. 1:8–10)

CHRONIC ILLNESS CAN bring you to desperate places. When symptoms of pain and illness increase, I can often push through for a while, but eventually I reach a breaking point. I want to give up. I've persevered for so long, and the thought of continuing forward feels like too much.

Do you ever reach a breaking point? Times when you don't know how you will survive to the end of the day? Sometimes it doesn't matter how hard you try; it's impossible to keep going. You can't stand up without fainting. You can't survive outside the hospital. The pain leaves you curled up in a fetal position in a dark corner of your bedroom. You are burdened beyond your own strength, and there is absolutely nothing you can do to save yourself.

At one point, the apostle Paul was on a missionary journey that made him feel this way. The situation was so bleak that he thought he was going to die. Paul believed that God brought him to this place so that he would stop trusting in his own strength and rely on God, who raises the dead. He describes God in this way to remind us of the Lord's power. God takes dead bodies and gives them life. He takes impossible situations and makes them possible (see Luke 1:37).

Paul was so certain of God's deliverance that he mentioned it three times. It can be difficult to share his assurance. We would rather be in a position where we can save ourselves. How do we put our hope in God when he may not show up in the way that we want? Chronic illness can and does destroy bodies, relationships, careers, happiness, and even lives. But the apostle makes an observation about God's character that is important for us to hear: because God has been faithful in the past, he will also be faithful in the future.

In desperate moments, it can feel impossible to hope in God. Yet, when we look back at hard times, we often wish we had trusted him more. I have never looked back over the years and thought, "God never showed up for me." He is always faithful. And the more times we experience his faithfulness, the more memories we have that remind us that we can rely on him in the present.

How about you? Has God been faithful to you as you've suffered? If so, you can trust that he won't stop. No matter the hardship you face, it isn't too much for him. He will give you everything you need to continue on into the future, no matter how impossible your situation might seem.

Reflect: Does life feel like more than you can handle? Don't try to get through on your own. Place your situation in God's hand. You can trust that he will be faithful.

Reflect: How has God been faithful to you in the past? How can remembering his past faithfulness help you to hope in him as you face current hardships?

DAY 30

Your Labor Is Not in Vain

Therefore, my dear brothers and sisters, be steadfast, immovable, always excelling in the Lord's work, because you know that your labor in the Lord is not in vain. (1 Cor. 15:58 CSB)

I LOVE THIS VERSE, because it reminds me that everything I do for the Lord matters. When chronic illness stops me in my tracks and all I can do is survive the day, there is still purpose and hope. There is reason to never give up. Maybe it seems like a stretch to gather this conclusion from one short verse, but stick with me for a moment.

This verse instructs us not to give up on the work of the Lord. This includes any work that you do in reliance on God and for his glory.[1] Any work that you do in this way, no matter how small, is not in vain. It won't result in nothing—which means that it must result in something.[2] Work for the Lord always bears fruit.

The reason for this is given earlier in 1 Corinthians 15 where Paul talks about the hope of the resurrection. Death has lost its sting. It doesn't have the final say. We have hope because Christ defeated death. One day Christ will return, the dead will be raised, and we will all be changed. Your perishable, mortal, weak body will be transformed into an imperishable and immortal body.

Work for the Lord is not in vain because Christ was resurrected, and one day you will be resurrected, too. Daily life with chronic illness can feel meaningless, but it has purpose that will last into eternity. Only grace can save you; but once you get to heaven, your past daily actions will matter. Your Spirit-empowered faithfulness is preparing you for glory (see 2 Cor. 4:16–18), and one day you will receive an inheritance from the Lord for all the work you have done for him (see Col. 3:23–24).

After heaven will come a new heaven and a new earth (see Rev. 21:1). When this happens, God won't destroy everything and start all over again. He will take all that there is and make it new (see Rev. 21:5). Your labor for the Lord is not in vain, because you are a part of this redemption process. One day, all the work you have done to better your body and soul will be a part of the "all things" that, even now, God is "making new." What's more, you have the ability to make that day come more quickly by living a holy and godly life (see 2 Peter 3:11–12).

No matter how tired or broken you feel, no matter how little you accomplish each day, no matter how meaningless or mundane your weeks and years feel—be encouraged. Your labor is not in vain. One day you will be rewarded. One day all that you have done will be made into something new. It is impossible to waste your life if you live it for God.

Reflect: What labors do you find yourself completing day after day? How can knowing that your labor is not in vain change your perspective on these daily tasks?

Act: Excel in the work of the Lord today. Make breakfast for the Lord. Take medication for the Lord. Do the dishes for the Lord. Take a nap for the Lord. Encourage a friend for the Lord. Control your anger for the Lord. Make someone tea for the Lord. Live all of life in reliance on God and for his glory, and one day you will see the fruit of your labor.

DAY 31

You Will Be Glorified

So we do not lose heart. Though our outer self is wasting away, our inner self is being renewed day by day. For this light momentary affliction is preparing for us an eternal weight of glory beyond all comparison. (2 Cor. 4:16–17)

HAVING A SERIOUS chronic illness is like being an Olympic athlete. Every day you make choices to bring your body to its peak performance ability. You move, rest, sleep, eat, take supplements, and complete treatments, all for the purpose of increasing your body's physical ability. Unfortunately, the comparison stops here; because most likely, you won't get the glory of competing in the Olympic games.

Instead, it's likely that your goal behind optimizing your body's performance is to do things such as shower, walk through the grocery store, and keep up with daily life. You go through all the pain for none of the glory. No one has any idea how hard you work, so there is no pat on the back for daily feats that seem mighty to you. There is no gold, silver, or bronze medal. No fame or recognition. No one gets flowers for chronic illness.

This is a depressing metaphor—but what if illness is preparing you for something far more glorious than the Olympic games? Scripture says that our afflictions are preparing an eternal weight of glory beyond all comparison. Somehow, in a process that is beyond our ability to fathom, suffering on earth leads to glorification in heaven.

Scripture describes the glorification you will experience in heaven using metaphors that are associated with royalty (see James 1:12). In heaven, God will recognize you and be pleased with you. Through chronic illness you share in Christ's suffering, and in heaven, the glory that has been given to Christ will be shared with you (see Rom. 8:17).

Scripture compares life to a race that might occur in a setting like the Olympic games (see Heb. 12:1). But this race isn't won by people who are at peak levels of fitness. No matter the state of our health, each of us can participate in what one pastor has called "Olympic spirituality."[1] This type of race is won not through physical strength but through "keeping the faith." We run this race not against "aging or physical deterioration" but against unbelief.[2]

This means that the race can be won and the glory can be yours even as your outer self wastes away. Even as your body declines, God is working a mysterious process of renewal inside you. He is giving you everything that you need to win as you lay aside weights and sins (see Heb. 12:1), look to Jesus (see Heb. 12:2), and maintain faith when you want to doubt (see 2 Tim. 4:7). When you win, you won't stand on a platform with a gold medal. The Lord himself will glorify you, awarding your faithfulness in Christ through chronic illness with a crown of righteousness (see 2 Tim. 4:8).

Don't lose heart. Chronic illness is preparing for you an eternal weight of glory that will make your current suffering seem like a grain of sand on a beach that spans all of eternity. Keep the faith. Fight doubt. Set aside sin. Run the race. One day you will hear God say, "Well done, good and faithful servant," as you enter into the joy of your master (Matt. 25:23).

Reflect: As you run toward glory, is your inner self being renewed? Are you keeping the faith? Are you setting aside weights and sins? Are you looking to Jesus?

Reflect: Imagine what it will be like to be glorified in heaven. Imagine what you will see and how you will feel. Imagine how it will all be worth it.

Conclusion

I'M LYING ON my couch with my laptop propped up on my knees as I type. This past weekend was the beginning of a flare, and I know I won't be doing much for the next few weeks. Months? I'm not sure at this point. Either way, it's discouraging, and I'm reminded that there is no "arriving" when you have chronic illness. The cycle of ups and downs never seems to end. It is exhausting, painful, and demoralizing to crash and fall over and over again. I don't feel completely at peace today, but I do feel a level of resolve. I have done this before, and I know I can do it again. It's easy to feel defeated, but deep down in my soul I find a mustard seed of faith. God is real. God is with me. He is at work.

Life with chronic illness isn't easy. We mourn our losses, only to realize a few months or years later that we need to mourn them yet again. Each day seems to reveal one more unexpected, inconvenient, painful way in which chronic illness impacts our lives. Most people don't escape chronic illness. Through all the ups and downs, we hold on for dear life, hoping and praying that God is doing something. Anything. Fulfilling some work or purpose that will make this all worthwhile.

Deep down I know that God is at work, and I hope that the Scriptures in this devotional illuminate some of what God is doing in and through the life you are living with chronic illness. Maybe you are now more aware of God's presence during your pain and feel more confident that he allows you to prioritize self-care. I hope you have been moved to consider how you can live purposefully with your illness and feel encouraged to not give up. However, even Scripture doesn't illuminate everything. Some questions about chronic illness remain unanswered.

There are secret things in life that belong to God alone (see

Deut. 29:29)—things too wonderful for us to know (see Job 42:3). While I am confident that God has a purpose for everything, his decisions often confound me. So much about chronic illness still doesn't make sense to me, and I'm sure you are left with unresolved wonderings of your own. Perhaps you can't fathom how a good God could allow you to endure unspeakable levels of pain. Maybe you wonder why God would make it physically impossible for you to care for your children. While God works through chronic illness in incredible ways, it's easy for us to question why he doesn't use less painful avenues to reach the same ends.

At the beginning of this book, I expressed my hope that you would be surprised by how much God has to say about chronic illness. That hope still stands. But I end this book on a different note. For as much as God reveals in his Word, we are still left to wrestle with all the things that he leaves unsaid.

During life on earth, "we see in a mirror dimly" (1 Cor. 13:12). Our understanding of life is like a distorted reflection bouncing back from an ancient mirror. On occasion God gives us a glimpse of his plan. For a moment we understand what he is doing, and a palpable sense of relief fills our souls. Unfortunately, these moments can feel few and far between.

It's painful to stumble through life with unanswered questions, but we won't always be left in the dark. First Corinthians 13:12 reads, in full, "For now we see in a mirror dimly, but then face to face. Now I know in part; then I shall know fully, even as I have been fully known." One day we will see God and live with him forever. We will know the Lord fully, just as he has fully known us through all the ups and downs of our illness. On that day, our questions will melt in his presence. We will begin new lives—lives that are free from sin, sickness, and pain.

Until then, walk forward in faith, and be confident that one day you will walk by sight (see 2 Cor. 5:7). One day you will be in the presence of the Lord, and God will open your eyes. You will see the things that you hope for. You will understand the things that don't make sense. Through all the ups and downs of life with illness, you will see that God was walking beside you this whole time.

Acknowledgments

WRITING THIS BOOK would not have been possible without my husband, Ian. Through sickness and more sickness, you have supported and encouraged me in countless ways. Thank you for all the ways you never give up on me.

Eliza, this book would not have happened without you. Thank you for believing in me and supporting my writing! Thank you to Deepak for taking the time to read my writing and for opening up this opportunity for me as a new writer. I am so grateful for all your encouragement and guidance along the way.

Thank you to those who supported me in various ways throughout the writing process. Natalie and Alison, thank you for your valuable feedback as I completed my initial drafts. To my sisters, Sarah and Heather, thank you for continually checking in and cheering me on. To my friend Christine, your support, encouragement, and feedback, and most of all your friendship, mean the world to me. So much of what I have learned about living a faithful life with chronic illness I have learned from you.

Over the years, I have interacted with many people who have chronic illness in various places—online and in person; in my counseling room, through my blog, and in various support groups. There are too many of you for me to mention, but you know who you are. To each and every one of you, thank you for walking with me, teaching me, and showing me that I am not alone.

Notes

Day 4: Say How Much It Hurts

1. See C. H. Spurgeon, *The Treasury of David*, vol. 2, *Psalm XXVII to LII* (New York, 1882), 62, quoted in David Guzik, "Psalm 31—Shelter from Trouble in the Secret Place of God's Presence," The Enduring Word Bible Commentary, accessed May 20, 2019, https://enduringword.com/bible-commentary/psalm-31/.

Day 5: Trust the Lord

1. See Corrie ten Boom with Elizabeth Sherrill and John Sherrill, *The Hiding Place*, 35th anniv. ed. (Grand Rapids: Chosen Books, 2011), chap. 12, Kindle.

Day 6: Look for God in Lonely Places

1. Dietrich Bonhoeffer, *Life Together*, trans. John W. Doberstein (1954; repr., London: SCM Press, 2010), chap. 1, Kindle.

2. See "ἔρημος," Blue Letter Bible, accessed May 20, 2019, https://www.blueletterbible.org/lang/lexicon/lexicon.cfm?Strongs=G2048&t=ESV, Strong's number G2048.

Day 7: When You Don't Know How to Pray

1. See Charles Spurgeon, "The Holy Spirit's Intercession" (sermon, Metropolitan Tabernacle, London, UK, April 11, 1880), available online at http://www.spurgeongems.org/vols25-27/chs1532.pdf.

Day 10: Take Care of Your Body

1. See N. T. Wright, *Surprised by Hope: Rethinking Heaven, the Resurrection, and the Mission of the Church*, reprint ed. (San Francisco: HarperOne, 2018), 193.

Day 12: Care for Yourself in Community

1. See note at *Vine's Greek New Testament Dictionary*, s.v. "burden, burdened, burdensome (A2)," accessed May 16, 2019, http://

gospelhall.org/bible/bible.php?search=phortion&dict=vine&
lang=greek.

Day 15: A Spiritual Struggle

1. See Leslie Vernick, *The Emotionally Destructive Relationship: Seeing It, Stopping It, Surviving It* (Eugene, OR: Harvest House, 2007), for information on this topic.

Day 17: Chronic Illness and Your Thoughts

1. See "λογίζομαι," Blue Letter Bible, accessed May 16, 2019, https://www.blueletterbible.org/lang/lexicon/lexicon.cfm?Strongs=G3049&t=ESV, Strong's number G3049.

Day 21: Stewards of God's Grace

1. Westminster Shorter Catechism, answer 1.

Day 24: Strength in Weakness

1. For a full discussion of this topic, see Henry Frost, *Miraculous Healing: Why Does God Heal Some and Not Others?* (Fearn, UK: Christian Focus Publications, 1999).

Day 30: Your Labor Is Not in Vain

1. See John Piper, "Labor for the Lord Is Never Lost," Look at the Book, Desiring God, September 6, 2016, https://www.desiringgod.org/labs/labor-for-the-lord-is-never-lost.

2. See "κενός," Blue letter Bible, accessed May 16, 2019, https://www.blueletterbible.org/lang/lexicon/lexicon.cfm?Strongs=G2756&t=KJV, Strong's number G2756.

Day 31: You Will Be Glorified

1. John Piper, "I Have Chronic Fatigue—How Do I Not Waste My Life?" Ask Pastor John, Desiring God, August 29, 2018, https://www.desiringgod.org/interviews/i-have-chronic-fatigue-how-do-i-not-waste-my-life.

2. Piper, "I Have Chronic Fatigue."

Suggested Resources
for the Journey

Power, P. B. *A Book of Comfort for Those in Sickness.* Reprint, Edinburgh, UK: Banner of Truth, 2018. [This book was first published in 1876, but its message still rings true today. If you want a short and relatable book that addresses some of chronic illness's most common struggles, this is a great place to start. The book shows readers how to find God's comfort when they are faced with physical pain, feelings of uselessness, feelings of unworthiness, envious thoughts, isolation, and many other relevant topics.]

Frankl, Sara, and Mary Carver. *Choose Joy: Finding Hope and Purpose When Life Hurts.* Reprint, New York: FaithWords, 2017. [After the author, Sara Frankl, passed away due to chronic illness, her friend, Mary Carver, compiled many of Sara's blog posts into this book. This book is both challenging and encouraging; it provides hope that it is possible to live a life of joy in the face of long-term physical suffering.]

Tada, Joni Eareckson. *A Place of Healing: Wrestling with the Mysteries of Suffering, Pain, and God's Sovereignty.* Reprint, Colorado Springs: David C. Cook, 2015. [This honest and thought-provoking book was written decades after Joni's paralyzing diving accident. Many years later, she found herself facing a new challenge in the form of severe chronic pain. Joni began processing her experience as she wrote this book, and the result is a candid and personal look at maintaining hope and faith when life gives you more than you can handle.]

Smith, Esther. *But God, Wouldn't I Be More Useful to You If I Were Healthy?* Scotts Valley, CA: CreateSpace, 2016. [Chronic illness can cause us significant limitation, leaving us to wonder why God would take away our ability to work and serve and contribute. It's easy for us to struggle with feelings of emptiness, purposelessness, and self-pity. This story-filled book explores how to live a life of guilt-free rest and purposeful service when chronic illness leaves you watching from the sidelines.]

The Biblical Counseling Coalition (BCC) is passionate about enhancing and advancing biblical counseling globally. We accomplish this through broadcasting, connecting, and collaborating.

Broadcasting promotes gospel-centered biblical counseling ministries and resources to bring hope and healing to hurting people around the world. We promote biblical counseling in a number of ways: through our *15:14* podcast, website (biblicalcounselingcoalition.org), partner ministry, conference attendance, and personal relationships.

Connecting biblical counselors and biblical counseling ministries is a central component of the BCC. The BCC was founded by leaders in the biblical counseling movement who saw the need for and the power behind building a strong global network of biblical counselors. We introduce individuals and ministries to one another to establish gospel-centered relationships.

Collaboration is the natural outgrowth of our connecting efforts. We truly believe that biblical counselors and ministries can accomplish more by working together. The BCC Confessional Statement, which is a clear and comprehensive definition of biblical counseling, was created through the cooperative effort of over thirty leading biblical counselors. The BCC has also published a three-part series of multi-contributor works that bring theological wisdom and practical expertise to pastors, church leaders, counseling practitioners, and students. Each year we are able to facilitate the production of numerous resources, including books, articles, videos, audio resources, and a host of other helps for biblical counselors. Working together allows us to provide robust resources and develop best practices in biblical counseling so that we can hone the ministry of soul care in the church.

To learn more about the BCC, visit biblicalcounselingcoalition.org.

Was this book helpful to you?
Consider writing a review online.
The author appreciates your feedback!

Or write to P&R at editorial@prpbooks.com
with your comments. We'd love to hear from you.